Bb TRUMPET

HOLIDAY FAVORITES

Solos and Band Arrangements
Correlated with Essential Elements® Band Me...

Arranged by ROBERT LONGFIELD, JOHNNIE VINSON, MICHAEL SWEENEY and PAUL LAVENDER

Welcome to Essential Elements Holiday Favorites! There are two versions of each selection in this versatile book. The SOLO version appears in the beginning of each student book. The FULL BAND arrangement of each song follows. The ONLINE RECORDINGS or PIANO ACCOMPANIMENT BOOK may be used as an accompaniment for solo performance. Use these recordings when playing solos for friends and family.

PLAYBACK+
Speed • Pitch • Balance • Loop

To access audio visit:
www.halleonard.com/mylibrary

Enter Code
8348-7927-5767-3183

ISBN 978-1-5400-2795-5

Copyright © 2018 by HAL LEONARD LLC
International Copyright Secured   All Rights Reserved

Visit Hal Leonard Online at
www.halleonard.com

00870013

Contact Us:
Hal Leonard
7777 West Bluemound Road
Milwaukee, WI 53213
Email: info@halleonard.com

In Europe contact:
Hal Leonard Europe Limited
42 Wigmore Street
Marylebone, London, W1U 2RN
Email: info@halleonardeurope.com

In Australia contact:
Hal Leonard Australia Pty. Ltd.
4 Lentara Court
Cheltenham, Victoria, 3192 Australia
Email: info@halleonard.com.au

AULD LANG SYNE

Bb TRUMPET
Solo

Words by ROBERT BURNS
Traditional Scottish Melody
Arranged by MICHAEL SWEENEY

Copyright © 2006 by HAL LEONARD CORPORATION
International Copyright Secured   All Rights Reserved

FELIZ NAVIDAD

Music and Lyrics by
JOSÉ FELICIANO
Arranged by PAUL LAVENDER

Bb TRUMPET
Solo

00870013

PARADE OF THE WOODEN SOLDIERS

B♭ TRUMPET
Solo

English Lyrics by BALLARD MacDONALD
Music by LEON JESSEL
Arranged by PAUL LAVENDER

Toy March

mf

< f mf

f

mf

f mf

f

GOOD KING WENCESLAS

B♭ TRUMPET
Solo

Words by JOHN M. NEALE
Music from PIAE CANTIONES
Arranged by ROBERT LONGFIELD

PAT-A-PAN
(Willie, Take Your Little Drum)

Bb TRUMPET
Solo

Words and Music by
BERNARD de la MONNOYE
Arranged by ROBERT LONGFIELD

Moderato

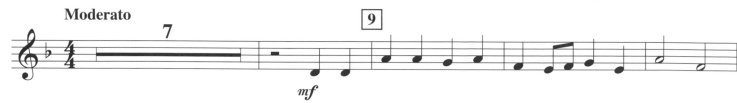

mf

lower notes opt.

opt. Play

Play

f

opt. Play

mf

p

SILVER BELLS

Bb TRUMPET
Solo

Words and Music by
JAY LIVINGSTON and RAY EVANS
Arranged by PAUL LAVENDER

00870013

DO YOU HEAR WHAT I HEAR

Bb TRUMPET
Solo

Words and Music by
NOEL REGNEY and GLORIA SHAYNE
Arranged by MICHAEL SWEENEY

00870013

From THE SOUND OF MUSIC

MY FAVORITE THINGS

Bb TRUMPET
Solo

Lyrics by OSCAR HAMMERSTEIN II
Music by RICHARD RODGERS
Arranged by ROBERT LONGFIELD

00870013

From the Motion Picture Irving Berlin's HOLIDAY INN

WHITE CHRISTMAS

B♭ TRUMPET
Solo

Words and Music by
IRVING BERLIN
Arranged by JOHNNIE VINSON

Moderate Tempo

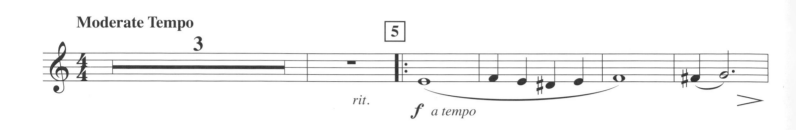

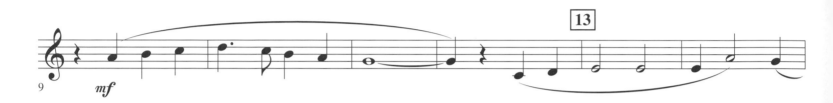

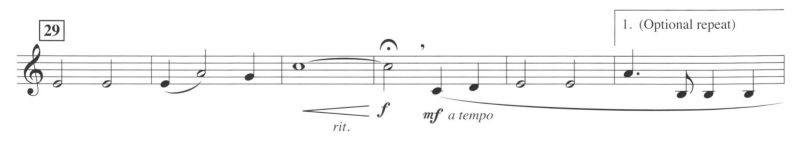

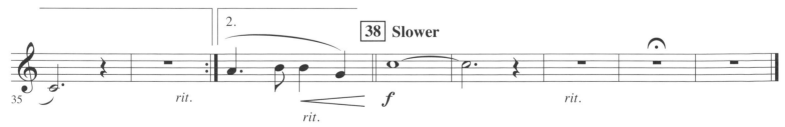

CHRISTMAS TIME IS HERE

Bb TRUMPET
SOLO

Words by LEE MENDELSON
Music by VINCE GUARALDI
Arranged by JOHNNIE VINSON

00870013

From Warner Bros. Pictures' THE POLAR EXPRESS

THE POLAR EXPRESS

B♭ TRUMPET
Solo

Words and Music by
GLEN BALLARD and ALAN SILVESTRI
Arranged by JOHNNIE VINSON

AULD LANG SYNE

B♭ TRUMPET
Band Arrangement

Words by ROBERT BURNS
Traditional Scottish Melody
Arranged by MICHAEL SWEENEY

00870013

FELIZ NAVIDAD

B♭ TRUMPET
Band Arrangement

Music and Lyrics by
JOSÉ FELICIANO
Arranged by PAUL LAVENDER

00870013

PARADE OF THE WOODEN SOLDIERS

B♭ TRUMPET
Band Arrangement

English Lyrics by BALLARD MacDONALD
Music by LEON JESSEL
Arranged by PAUL LAVENDER

00870013

GOOD KING WENCESLAS

B♭ TRUMPET
Band Arrangement

Words by JOHN M. NEALE
Music from PIAE CANTIONES
Arranged by ROBERT LONGFIELD

PAT-A-PAN
(Willie, Take Your Little Drum)

B♭ TRUMPET
Band Arrangement

**Words and Music by
BERNARD de la MONNOYE**
Arranged by ROBERT LONGFIELD

00870013

SILVER BELLS

B♭ TRUMPET
Band Arrangement

**Words and Music by
JAY LIVINGSTON and RAY EVANS**
Arranged by PAUL LAVENDER

DO YOU HEAR WHAT I HEAR

B♭ TRUMPET
Band Arrangement

Words and Music by
NOEL REGNEY and GLORIA SHAYNE
Arranged by MICHAEL SWEENEY

From THE SOUND OF MUSIC

MY FAVORITE THINGS

B♭ TRUMPET
Band Arrangement

Lyrics by OSCAR HAMMERSTEIN II
Music by RICHARD RODGERS
Arranged by ROBERT LONGFIELD

From the Motion Picture Irving Berlin's HOLIDAY INN

WHITE CHRISTMAS

Words and Music by
IRVING BERLIN
Arranged by JOHNNIE VINSON

B♭ TRUMPET
Band Arrangement

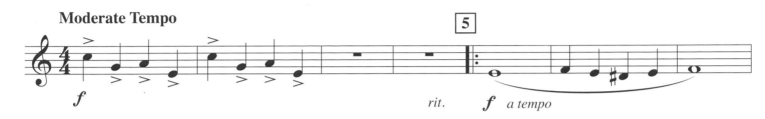

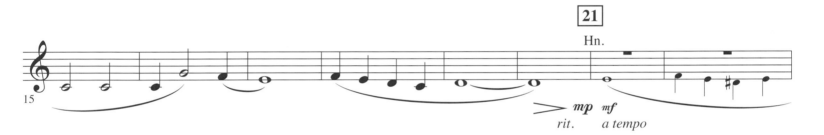

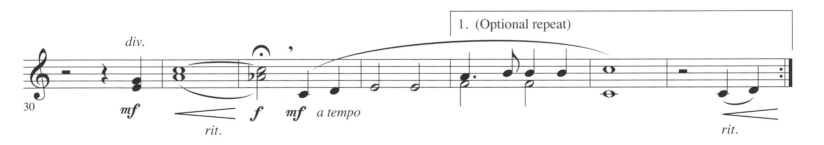

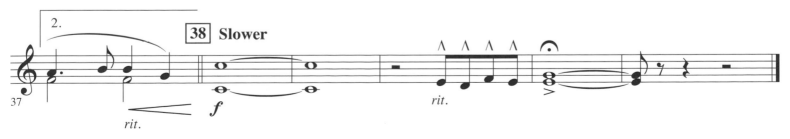

CHRISTMAS TIME IS HERE

B♭ TRUMPET
Band Arrangement

Words by LEE MENDELSON
Music by VINCE GUARALDI
Arranged by JOHNNIE VINSON

THE POLAR EXPRESS

Bb TRUMPET
Band Arrangement

Words and Music by
GLEN BALLARD and ALAN SILVESTRI
Arranged by JOHNNIE VINSON

00870013